What The "4 Chef" Didn't Tell You!

By Chef Marty Richardson

Learn To Prepare Mouth Watering Meals
...Without A Single Recipe

Mmmmm...Good!

More Information:
Visit http://ChefMartyRich.com
Individual Sales, Consultation, Speaking Events
Contact Chef Marty Rich
Quantity sales: Special discounts are available on quantity purchases by corporations, associations, and others. For details, contact the author at
http://ChefMartyRich.com

Publisher's Cataloging-in-Publication data

Richardson, Marty

What the "4-Hour Chef" Didn't Tell You! - Learn to Prepare Mouth Watering Meals Without a Single Recipe written by Marty Richardson
p. cm.

ISBN 978-1479221035
1. Cooking 2. Methods 3. Quick and Easy
I. Marty,Richardson. II. Title.

First Edition

ISBN-13:978-1492882442
ISBN-10:1492882445

Book cover and interior illustrations by Biz Technologies
Book design and production by Biz Technologies
http://bizbin.biz

DEDICATION

This book is dedicated to my loving parents, George and Alice, who instilled the confidence and independence in my brother Michael and I, to pursue our dreams, wherever in the world they may take us.

"Nothing great was ever achieved without enthusiasm"

Ralph Waldo Emerson

TABLE OF CONTENTS

QUICK START

If you only read one chapter, you must read this one, especially if you usually skip the introduction!

Learning By Recipes Will Make You A Bad Cook!

Would you agree that your favorite foods stimulate all your senses? It's more than the delicious taste you remember! Just inhaling the aroma draws you straight into the kitchen, as you hear the sizzle, snap, crackle and pop. Then you see the dish and it makes your mouth water in anticipation and finally, you feel the satisfying texture of a perfect chew. Remember?

If you learn to cook using taste, smell, sound, sight, and touch, then you will quickly produce food worthy of compliments. If your head is buried in a cookbook, you are not paying attention to what's happening on the stove. Recipes become useful only after you learn how to cook. Trust your senses!

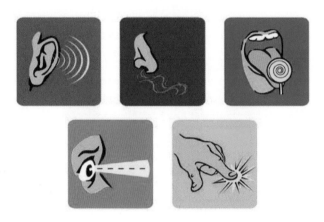

Most people probably grab a cookbook and learn by trial and (mostly) error. Unless circumstances force you to learn to cook, you will likely quit out of frustration. You may have already tried and quit before.

Each recipe has several ingredients you must buy, requires tools and equipment that you don't own, and uses terminology you don't understand. You ask for help and everyone is an "expert" with a different opinion. And how does someone who doesn't even know how to cook, become a food critic?!

Recipes don't teach you how to cook! In fact, they assume that you already know how to cook. If every recipe was written for a beginner, it would have so many steps that you would not know where to begin. The purpose of a recipe is to explain how to create unique flavors by combining ingredients and methods of preparation, *based on the author's palate.*

The sooner you trust your own taste buds, the faster you will make progress. The sooner you understand how to choose the best produce by weight and feel, the faster you will progress. When you learn to smell when something is beginning to burn, the faster you will progress.

When you start to notice when food is done cooking by sight, the faster you will make progress. And yes, even identifying sounds is an important skill in your culinary development. This is how great cooks are made!

A recipe, by definition, "is a list of ingredients and a set of instructions that tell you how to cook something". In practical terms, a recipe shows you how to "develop layers of flavor" by combining ingredients and methods of preparation. If you skip the first step, learning to cook, it is much more difficult to interpret and execute someone else's recipe.

Recipes do not follow a standardized format. **Not every recipe you read has been tested.** There is not a glossary in every cookbook you buy that explains the terminology the author uses.

Even if the recipe comes with a picture, how often does the dish look anything like that? Unless you know the author/cook, you will never know what the original dish looked like, tasted like, or smelled like. This is no way to learn a new skill.

Can you learn to cook from recipes? Yes you can. Most people do. It's the hard way. **This "cookbook" will show you the easiest way to becoming a great cook quickly without a single recipe.** The secret is to minimize beginner's mistakes and maximize early successes that inspire compliments, which in turn, will motivate you to cook more.

One of my favorite animated movies is "Ratatouille". If you have not seen it, I recommend it. Remy, a country rat, with a highly developed sense of smell and taste, learns to cook, and finds himself "cooking" in a 3 Star Paris restaurant. Early in the movie Remy tastes a mushroom after he (and the mushroom) is struck by lightning, and he is thrilled by the accidental discovery. He followed no recipe, just **ONE** ingredient and **ONE** (unconventional) source of heat.

Later, while trying to escape from Gusteau's kitchen, Remy runs through the steaming vapors of a soup pot on the stove. The smell stops him in his tracks, and he can't help adding ingredients to fix the soup. His cooking skill is immediately recognized by a food critic and the chef, which spurs him on to help his friend Linguini to cook. Again, Remy cooks by smell, without a recipe. (By the way, he never tastes food meant for human consumption! He's cute, but still a rat.)

In another scene, he is sharing grapes and cheese with his brother Emile, and trying to show him how to appreciate the flavor of each ingredient separately and how the combination is more than the sum of the two.

This is an important lesson for you to learn in time, and does not require a recipe. Remy's decision to change Chef Gusteau's "Anchovy-Licorice Sauce" for the Sweetbread recipe, transformed a dish that even the Chef did not like, into a raving success. It was his interpretation of the recipe that showcased his cooking style. **When you know how to cook, a recipe is merely a guide, not the training manual.**

The real test of Remy's ability came when food critic Anton Ego came to review "his" food. He chose a simple peasant dish, ratatouille, to serve. Just one taste and Mr. Ego was transported back to his childhood, remembering how comforting his mother's ratatouille tasted.

What dish brings you back to a particular time and place? Or is it a certain smell that really gets to you? **My point is that sensory experiences are cataloged in your brain for life.** If you don't like the ones you have, create new ones!

You can make an instant, lasting, emotional connection to another person, at a sensory level, with food. That is a powerful experience. Why not learn to cook using these same 5 senses? Great cooking is not about finding recipes with fancy pants ingredients and complicated methods of preparation. **Great food stimulates your senses and your imagination.** It is incredibly gratifying to share it with others.

"What do I always say? Anyone can cook!"
Chef Gusteau, from Ratatouille.

He had assumed a cookbook would come with a cook.

You can do this! In fact, you might find my method too simple in the beginning. You may have missed the method because it is so simple, so I will restate it again. Start by taking **ONE** raw ingredient and applying **ONE** method of heating until that ingredient is finished cooking to your desired doneness.

If you can do that, you can cook. Of course cooking can get infinitely more complicated, but it doesn't have to! Stop convincing yourself, and others, that you can't cook. I am going to show you how.

Be sure to go to http://ChefMartyRich.com/book-bonus/ and receive your ***Secret Ingredients to Successful Cooking.***

Let's Get Started!

WARNING! IF YOU DID NOT READ THE QUICK START, GO BACK AND READ IT NOW! YOU MAY NOT UNDERSTAND THE REST OF THIS BOOK IF YOU DON'T READ IT FIRST! SERIOUSLY…READ IT!

CHAPTER 1

"The 4 Hour Chef" Is <u>NOT</u> Going To Teach You How To Cook!!!"

The 3 time New York Times best-selling author Timothy Ferriss has written a massive (671 page) book, "The 4-Hour Chef" about "Learning Anything". The subtitle reads *"The simple path to cooking like a pro, learning anything, and living the good life."* Strike One! Strike Two! Strike Three? Although the book is crammed with recipes and step-by-step photos, the very first sentence is a disclaimer that it isn't a cookbook.

Just skimming through the book will convince you that his methods are anything but simple. For the past month I've tried to learn how to use his book! The reason why "Strike Three" has a question mark is that I don't know how he defines "living the good life". It could be that his message is just beyond me at this time.

Truth be told, it's a beautiful book, and I was sold on the title alone.

I'm a Ferriss Fan, and a career Chef, so I was excited to buy the book. Who wouldn't want to learn from "the most interesting man in the world"? This guy is intense! He dedicates his body to medical research. He speaks 6 languages. He is a Guinness Book of World's Record holder in tango spinning. He is a Chinese kickboxing champion. And he is an angel investor! The man exudes confidence and is a master of self-promotion.

If you are reading his book to learn how to cook, the one thing you probably don't have is confidence in your culinary abilities. If you did not grow up learning at your Mother's side, like I did, and decided to start cooking later in life, then it is easy to get frustrated in the kitchen.

How do you think you would perform if you just decided to start singing or dancing tomorrow? Isn't that why we watch "American Idol" and "Dancing with the Stars"? Do you think you could handle the criticism? Isn't it easier to watch from home and poke fun at the contestants? **Do you think it would be easy to learn to sing or dance from a book?** Is it any different to learn to cook?

My point is that we put a lot of pressure on people (and ourselves) to perform. Cooking is no different. Either we expect value (good flavor, big portions and friendly service) for our money, or we accept less, as long as we know exactly what we are getting (Number 2 with a Diet Coke). We all expect a certain level of perfection, but don't you think you can make a better hamburger than McDonalds?

So how was your cooking debut? Are your friends and family still laughing at/with you? Is that the reason why you don't cook? It is well documented how much training the contestants on DWTS go through before the cameras start rolling. **Did you think you were going to teach yourself how to cook without a coach?**

Mr. Ferriss had a decided advantage in his quest to learn how to cook. He had access to some of the world's greatest chefs and restaurants due to his level of notoriety. By the end of the book, I'm still not convinced that he learned how to cook or whether he learned to follow a recipe. They are two different skills. And where do the 4 hours fit into the equation? It's very clever branding!

I can't say that I agree with the conclusion that his accelerated method of learning how to cook, "teaches you to become fully conscious and aware of the incredible things you *already* have." The book would be far less interesting without the step-by-step photos of gutting and dressing a deer, making arugula spaghetti or knowing which "tactical" knives are preferred by trained killers. However, I do agree with him on this. Chasing after money may not solve all your problems, but sharing a home cooked meal with family and friends, "just might".

"If you really want to make a friend, go to someone's house and eat with him... the people who give you their food give you their heart." Cesar Chavez

CHAPTER 2

There's More Than One Way To Skin A Cat...

OK, maybe that isn't the most appropriate chapter title for a book on learning how to cook, but here's what I mean. While reading The 4 Hour Chef, I could not help but think of how I would try to teach someone how to cook in just 4 hours. My first thought was "impossible". There are so many tricks and tips to know and after 30 years of cooking professionally, I'm still learning! Then I realized that I started by cooking simple food, and then I became hungry for knowledge and my cooking got very complex.

Now my cooking style has come full circle, back to simple. In the beginning, simple cooking reflected my skills and knowledge. The more I learned about food, the more I applied. I began "flexing" my knowledge of ingredients and international cuisines. Later, **I came to understand that quality ingredients prepared simply, was the secret.** It is enjoyed by more people and it is easier to make!

I decided to write this book in response to "The 4-Hour Chef". I believe that after you learn a skill, it's your responsibility to teach. Most chefs spend more time teaching their staff to consistently produce quality dishes, than actually cooking themselves. Many other people taught me and I want to share my knowledge with you.

So, in these pages, I will offer my condensed philosophy and practice on learning how to cook. **If you enjoy what you read, I will give you an opportunity to learn more in an interactive,**

online cooking class. This book is where you should begin. <u>This is</u> **NOT** a cookbook! There are **NO** <u>recipes, so you will not be</u> <u>confused.</u>

This is the basic information you need to know, BEFORE you start cooking. If you understand my approach, your chances of achieving of initial successes will be greatly enhanced. "STEAK TIPS" will highlight the most important points. If you have questions or suggestions for a second edition, email me at chefmartyrich@gmail.com.

"If you think you can or you think you can't… you are right." Henry Ford

You may not know how to cook…or you may SAY that you don't know how to cook. It's all about mindset. Basic cooking is really not hard. With just a few tips and tricks, you can easily make satisfying meals for yourself, family and friends.

If you convince yourself you can't cook, and a dish does not come out the way you expected, you find validation and frustration. I have cooked for over 30 years and I still make mistakes. Cut yourself some slack. It's just a part of the process. Occasionally, a "mistake" will improve a dish. Once you get over this mental hurdle, cooking becomes easier. It's actually a lot of fun to experiment!

Early in his book, Mr. Ferriss included a section about "Why You Will Succeed – Two Principles". He said that all learning comes down to **failure points** and the **margin of safety**. He outlines 6 failure points (reasons/excuses) why people put cookbooks down. I interpret the failure points as the reason why people stop cooking. He compiled this list from a Facebook poll of over 100,000 of his fans.

Ferriss's Failure Points

- **Too many ingredients (too much shopping and too much prep)**

- **Intimidating knife skills, introduced too early in the cookbook**

- **Too many tools, pots, and pans which are expensive and require cleaning**

- **Food spoilage**

- **Different dishes finishing at different times**

- **Dishes that require constant tending, stirring and watching**

He believes that the primary goal of a novice cook should be to overcome these failure points to become a better cook. I will address each of these points in detail, later in this book. Each failure point can be overcome with a little education, except maybe the last point. Most dishes do require your attention, especially when you are learning. No apologies offered.

The second principle is margin of safety, which he describes as the quality of the recipe. Finding a cookbook that you have confidence in is a beautiful thing, and another exercise in trial and error.

Unfortunately, a novice is in no position to judge the quality of its recipes and is therefore at the mercy of the cookbook. I have been involved in the production of a cookbook, and I can tell you that rarely are all the recipes tested!

I don't think you should start learning to cook from recipes. When you are cooking from a book, your attention is naturally divided between the cookbook and the meal. Things get infinitely complicated if you are cooking more than one new dish at the same meal! You probably don't even have the room to keep two books open at the same time on your kitchen counter while you are cooking!

My point is that simple food, cooked simply is easy and can be learned in a few hours. You can spend a lifetime making it more complicated and experimenting with different ethnic variations, but when you master these few skills, you are good to go!

Again, let me say that this is not a cookbook. Although Mr. Ferriss also claims that, his book is full of recipes, so it is easily mistaken for a cookbook! **This is a "learn to cook" book.** I believe recipes are important, but if you don't understand the basics about food, shopping and methods of preparation, then recipes are no guarantee of success.

Be sure to go to http://ChefMartyRich.com/book-bonus/ and receive your *Secret Ingredients to Successful Cooking*

"Recipes are important but only to a point. What's more important than recipes is how we think about food, and a good cookbook should open up a new way of doing just that." Michael Symon

CHAPTER 3

So Who Am I, And Why Should You Listen To Me?

My love affair with food began at an early age. I was born in Boston, Massachusetts, and when I was five, my family moved from the city, to a little country town called West Bridgewater. Even at that age, it was a complete culture shock. We had about five acres of land, some of it was wooded, but most of it was already cleared. Before long, we had small farm with vegetable gardens, a pony, pigs and chickens.

As cliché as it sounds, there's a lot of work to farming. I don't remember that being part of the deal when we asked for the pony! The chores never seemed to end, even in the winter. It was also incredibly rewarding to eat the "fruits of your labor". It was easier to eat the vegetables, than the chickens or pigs. It's all fun and games until it's time to eat your "pet". Some lessons were hard to learn.

I can still remember pulling a carrot out of the ground and just wiping it off on my pants and eating it. To this day, I've never tasted anything sweeter, grit and all, it was great. We would have to pick green beans, strawberries, tomatoes and cucumbers twice a day, just to keep up. Imagine picking corn off the stalk and putting it in the pot less than five minutes later. **There's nothing like growing your own food.**

The other "hunter-gatherer" activity we depended on when I was younger was fishing. Out of our back door and through the woods and across the Foye's field was the Town River. We did a lot of fishing and there was no such thing as "catch and release"! We grew up with a different understanding of the expression, "bringing home the bacon".

It's amazing that we have access to almost every food, all year round. In the southern hemisphere, our winter is their summer growing season, and because of improved transportation, we have fresh (summer) fruits – peaches, melons, blueberries and strawberries all winter long.

Check the labels on your produce the next time you are in the grocery store. More and more is being imported to supplement our diet, and keep the produce shelves full.

I will fast forward through the Boy Scout campfire meals eaten in aluminum mess kits, and the freeze dried meals while hiking down the Appalachian Trail. No need to discuss grilling at the summer bachelor pad during college, but I will give a quick mention to the post graduate, "semi-homemade" days when I was first on my own.

Sometimes it takes a woman's touch (and encouragement) before you start cooking indoors in a proper kitchen. I soon became a master of semi-homemade cooking long before Sandra Lee made it to the Food Network. I can still remember my first successful dinner party. The menu included a Purdue Oven Stuffer Roaster with Stovetop Stuffing, Green Giant frozen corn, (real) mashed potatoes, Pepperidge Farms Crescent Rolls and Duncan Hines Brownies topped with Vanilla Ice Cream. That sense of pride stuck with me a long time!

I want you to experience the same feeling. That is the reason I still cook today. Pride will give you with the motivation to stick with it when you make mistakes. I believe in "The Joy of Cooking" and so will you, when you get better at it. I am not a "food snob". It is important that you cook to **your** standards and taste, not mine.

If it is easier for you to supplement your cooking with processed foods to get you going, then so be it. You will soon learn that your version, made from scratch, tastes better and is better for you. **The sooner you prepare food that you enjoy eating, the more often you will want to cook and the faster your skills will improve.**

NOTES

CHAPTER 4

A Harvard Grad Walks Into A Golf Course Snack Bar...

Little did I know that my professional food service career would start a year later in Newport, RI. Oh boy, my father was not pleased! I was supposed to be a doctor, a lawyer, or an Indian Chief...but a short order cook? I loved hearing compliments on my cooking, but this was not his idea of a suitable career choice.

I was happy and satisfied that my customers were happy and satisfied. Cooking at the Green Valley Country Club changed my life! On Fridays, we would serve Snow's Clam Chowder, right out of the can. One day we were running kind of low, so I added some potatoes and milk to the last can of clam chowder to stretch it. Everybody was amazed at the result, thinking I had made it from scratch. The response was overwhelming.

My roommate, Crazy Mike and I were eating lunch at a restaurant called "Yesterdays". I remember saying that I need to start working at a more serious restaurant because I think I really like cooking. Later that day, I answered a blind ad in the newspaper, and it turned out to be Yesterdays! It was a sign!

This was my first job in a real restaurant. Everything from soup to dessert was made from scratch. We served daily specials for lunch and dinner, which exposed me to a wide variety of ingredients and different methods of preparation. The more I learned, the more I wanted to learn.

I was promoted from the grill position to other jobs throughout the kitchen until I became a Sous Chef ("second in command") in less than two years. I literally studied my craft. Every day, I went to the library and read cookbooks cover to cover. Just reading through them increased my understanding of ingredients and how different cultures prepared the same ingredients in different ways. I learned about flavor combinations, and how to make all the famous dishes.

When I visited Europe, and tasted food from different countries, I realized how important food is to each culture. Since then, I've worked from Rhode Island and Massachusetts to Alaska, Hawaii and Colorado, and from Florida and the Caribbean, to Southeast Asia and all over Western Europe including Italy, Spain, France, Germany, and England.

After 8 years of cooking, I went to Johnson and Wales University and earned a Culinary Degree. When I started classes, I thought I already knew "everything". I soon realized that it wasn't possible to know everything about food. More than 20 years later, I'm still learning, happily. **Now, I am confident that I can teach you enough practical knowledge to get you started in the kitchen in about four hours.** After that, you have the rest of your life to practice!

The lives of most people around the world revolve around food. Their day is mostly consumed with finding food, preparing food, eating and moving onto the next meal. Their existence is all about survival. For most of us in the United States, our lives are not "consumed" by wondering where your next meal is coming from. More often, the biggest challenge we seem to have is choosing which type of food we want to eat.

What is your relationship with food? Do you have a favorite meal or cherished memories that involve food? What was Thanksgiving like at your house? Are you starting or quitting a diet? Do you just want to have a few friends over or cook a meal for your family and sit together at the table for a change? I hope this book inspires you to develop a friendly relationship with food and cooking, one meal at a time. Enjoy! Be sure to go to http://ChefMartyRich.com/book-bonus/ and receive your *Secret Ingredients to Successful Cooking*

"80% of success is just showing up!"
Woody Allen

NOTES

CHAPTER 5

6 Reasons To Continue Reading This Book, Especially If You Have Quit Trying To Learn How To Cook

#1) I will show you how to buy the best ingredients, treat them simply, and let their flavors win you praise. The more you know about your ingredients, the easier it is to shop and the better your finished dishes. **Shopping is as important as cooking!**

#2) It is easier to learn to cook BEFORE you start using recipes! Knowing how to cook meat, fish, chicken and vegetables properly, using different methods of preparation is the foundation to ensure your success.

#3) If you are just getting started, **DO NOT go out and buy an expensive set of pots and pans.** Start with what you have. I will show you how to determine what equipment to buy and where to buy it.

#4) Cooking techniques or methods of preparation may be the most challenging aspect of cooking. What method are you going to use to heat your food? They are relatively easy to describe, but take practice to master.

#5) Are you frustrated because different dishes are never done at the same time? **I will show you how to use your oven or microwave timer to get all the food on the table at the same time.**

#6) Clean. Separate. Cook. Chill. I will share four simple ways for you to control food-borne illnesses in your home, whether you cook or not.

I will cover all this information, and much, much more… If you follow the simple steps, you will be hearing compliments on your food in no time. In fact, you can get started with just a few hours a week! **Check out my "STEAK TIPS" found in boxes throughout the book.** I will include helpful resources for you to reference in Chapter 18.

The point of this book is to help you experience the same joy and satisfaction that I get from cooking…from the beginning. Your kitchen confidence will grow from early successes, based on the knowledge you will learn on the remaining pages. Slow and steady wins the race. Be patient. **Start with one dish at a time, once or twice a week.**

I will give you enough information, so when you close this book, you'll be able to go into the supermarket and kitchen with a little more confidence. You will be inspired to try something new, and get enough compliments to make you want to go back in and try something else.

This is the formula that got me interested in cooking professionally and the same reasons why I still enjoy so many years later. The formula is universal. I have cooked my way around the world and "breaking bread" is the most powerful connector between people, even if you don't speak their language!

Be sure to go to http://ChefMartyRich.com/book-bonus/ and receive your *Secret Ingredients to Successful Cooking*

"Julia Child wasn't afraid to have fun. She made fantastic food but knew how to have a good time and not be too stuck up about the kitchen space." Nadia Giosia

CHAPTER 6

Shop often, shop hard, and spend for the best stuff available - logic dictates that you can make delicious food only with delicious ingredients. Mario Batali

Don't be intimidated by food. I understand if you are just starting, there are a lot of unusual textures and smells, but it's not "dirty". It's just food. You probably have food that you have always avoided. You may not want to eat fish. Either you don't like the way it feels, or smells. Maybe you don't want to touch shrimp or eat liver. It's all kind of weird, but it's just food. Okay? Most of it won't bite back!

The most important thing in cooking (after confidence) is the ingredients. What are you going to cook? **My philosophy is simple. Buy the best ingredients you can and try not to cover up their flavors.** If you start out with poor quality ingredients, you have to be a magician in the kitchen to prepare a high quality meal. Maybe you have heard the expression, "Garbage in…garbage out".

A great tomato does all the work for you! If you just slice it, and serve it, you can let its flavor be the star, and you get all the credit! Of course, you can sprinkle on a little sea salt and some fresh cracked black pepper, or drizzle on some aged balsamic vinegar and extra virgin olive oil and layer it with fresh buffalo mozzarella and basil, but the star of the dish is still the great tomato.

> **"Simple ingredients, treated with respect... put them together and you will always have a great dish."**
> **Jose Andres Puerta**

We all have access to different levels of quality ingredients, depending upon where we live. You may live on a farm and grow it yourself, or you may live in a metropolitan area and we have access to six different supermarkets in a four mile radius, or you may live in the Florida Panhandle, like I do. For us, the closest supermarket ("The Piggly Wiggly") is about a half hour drive away.

Understand that supermarkets are "super marketers". You are being manipulated from the moment you drive into the parking lot. I'm sure you know not to shop hungry, to bring a list, and that the perishables are along the perimeter. Just try to shop consciously. Supplement your produce purchases at a Farmer's Market. It's great to know where your food is coming from, while reinvesting in your community.

You have to do the best you can with the level of quality you have access to, or you can afford. Maybe you've got a Whole Foods organic food store nearby, but can't afford it, don't sweat it. There are many factors involved in sourcing your groceries, but the bottom line is simply, buy the best food that you can find/afford and treat it simply.

I realize that for many of you, "shopping" is one reason you avoid cooking. Some people don't like to shop for food, but if you are going to cook, it is an important errand. If I am planning a menu, I go to the store first and see what looks good first, rather than deciding on a menu first and getting frustrated when I can't find the right ingredients.

When I worked on a private yacht in Malaysia, supermarkets were far and few in between. Most people shopped in open air marketplaces. My first few visits to the market were unsettling, coming from the States.

There were flies everywhere and dogs with mange running around. During the rainy season, there were streams flowing down the aisles and the only source of refrigeration was melting ice. We all have our level of comfort or discomfort, as it were. I had to just get over it!

Later, I found that most people in that area didn't own a refrigerator. A significant number of people in the world don't have refrigeration, which is something we take for granted. The locals go to a marketplace two or three times a day and buy only what they need for each meal. There are no leftovers. If they only need a couple of cauliflower florets, and six shrimp, then that's all they buy.

Everything was sold individually. You go with a little basket and get all the ingredients you need for breakfast, and then go back to the market for lunch and then go back for dinner. Their life revolved around the marketplace…one meal at a time. In the United States, the packaging often determines how much we buy and how often we shop.

While you are at the store, make sure that your pantry is well stocked. There was a time when people actually had a pantry or a root cellar in the basement where you would store the root vegetables (onions, carrots, potatoes) and canned goods. Your pantry should be stocked with dried and canned goods that have a relatively long shelf life.

The biggest benefit of a well-stocked pantry is that you don't have to go to the grocery store every time you want to cook a meal.

Your pantry might just be a couple cabinets in your kitchen, or you might be lucky enough to have a closet-sized pantry where all this food and drink can be stored at room temperature. Grow your pantry with a few items at a time. **Stock up on the items you think you will use the most when they are on sale.**

My pantry list is going to be different from yours. Build your pantry with the ingredients you like and will use. If you don't like black beans, or if you have no intention of baking fresh bread, then leave black beans and yeast off your list.

Resist the urge to buy a complete set of herbs and spices. Very few cooks use more than half of the seasonings in those collections. Dried herbs and spice will start to lose their flavor after 6 months to a year. Buy small containers of the ones you already know that you like and the ones necessary for a recipe you want to make. You will soon discover the ones you use all the time. Buy those in larger quantities.

"Find combinations of flavors you love and buy the best quality ingredients you can afford. Your food is only going to be as good as the sum of its parts, like anything else." Gail Simmons

NOTES

CHAPTER 7

Vegetables are interesting but lack a sense of purpose when unaccompanied by a good cut of meat.
Fran Lebowitz

Disclaimer: If you chose not to eat or cook meat, I understand. You may want to skip ahead to Chapter 10.

Throughout my childhood, we raised animals to eat. I have always been aware that each part of the process, from purchase to diet to slaughter to packaging, influenced the meat that we ate. I also owned Vaillancourt's Meat Market for about four years beginning in 2001. So, meat has been at the center of the plate for my entire life.

Meat is usually the most expensive item on your menu. Knowing which cut to buy can sometimes be a problem, even for an experienced cook, but it doesn't have to be. **If you are lucky enough to have a meat market or butcher shop in your vicinity, I would suggest you use it.** The butcher may seem to be more expensive at first and it may require you to make another stop, but when you have time (or a special occasion) check it out.

There is a pronounced difference between a butcher and the meat cutter at your local supermarket. It is rare to find someone working in the supermarket meat department that is as knowledgeable as a butcher when it comes to helping you pick the right cuts of meat, giving advice on how to cook those cuts, and ordering specialty cuts for you. You will save money in the long run because you will be better educated about the meat you buy.

Imagine this scenario… You come into my meat market looking to buy a steak and I start "peppering" you with questions. "How many people are you serving? Do you like/dislike fat? How are you going to cook it? Will each person have their own steak or will you slice it and let them serve themselves? How much money would you like to spend? I had so many questions for people that they were probably thinking, "I just want a steak, not the Spanish Inquisition!"

So, why did I ask all those questions? The answers will lead us to the best steak for you on that occasion. **Different steaks come from different parts of a cow, which means they taste different, they cook different, they have different fat content and they are priced accordingly**.

A good butcher will help you navigate to the right steak. This process is further complicated in the supermarket, because they cut and package "steaks" out of primal parts that are not good for steak. They are only good for sales!

This is not common knowledge. Many people figure this out by accident, and then always use the same cut. The more you know about each cut, the more options you have when it comes to planning your menu. As an example, I want to take you back to my butcher shop and talk about beef steaks.

There are many different cuts labeled "steak", but for the purpose of this discussion, I want to focus on 5 popular steaks (tenderloin/filet, rib-eye, NY Strip, top sirloin and flank steak). These are some of the factors I consider when picking the right steak.

"Beef. It's What's For Dinner." The Beef Council

Beef Tenderloin

First, I ask how many people you are serving. The tenderloin, rib-eye and NY strip are the most expensive cuts per pound, so if you are feeding a crowd, it is going to cost you a small fortune...even at Costco.

The top sirloin and flank steak are cheaper per pound and can be cooked in larger pieces and served sliced. **There is much less wasted meat when each guest can control their portion size.**

Rib Eye Steak

41

Then, I ask if you are trying to avoid fat. **Many people are trying to reduce the amount of animal fat they eat.** It is important to know that "with fat comes flavor". **The less fat in the muscle, the less is tastes like beef.** Tenderloin has virtually no fat and is wonderfully tender, but has the least amount of beef flavor among these steaks.

A rib-eye has fat marbled throughout the muscle, which makes it tender and flavorful. It is the best steak in my opinion, but it is hard to avoid the fat. On the other hand, the marbling on a NY strip is more evenly distributed, and the majority of the fat is on the outside of the muscle, meaning it can be easily cut off after cooking. It is easy to trim the fat from the top sirloin and the flank steak as well.

NY Strip Steak

How are you going to cook it? The tenderloin is the most versatile cut of the group. It is great for grilling, roasting, broiling sautéing, and stir-frying. The rib-eye has fat pockets that will melt and cause flare ups if you are grilling. That's not a bad thing, as long as someone is constantly tending the grill. Because of the size of the steaks, you probably cannot cook more than two rib-eyes or NY strips, if you are pan frying on the stove. The top sirloin and flank steak are much larger still and better suited for grilling and broiling, unless you cut them into smaller pieces before cooking.

Flank Steak

Because of the relative size of each individual steak, I ask if each person will have their own steak, or be served slices. As described above, the rib-eye, and the NY strip are usually served whole and the top sirloin and flank steak best served in slices. The tenderloin can be cut and cooked for one or many.

Top Sirloin

Lastly, how much money do you want to spend? Is this a special occasion, or just a family backyard BBQ? You may or may not be thinking of all these things while you are considering which steak to buy, but obviously there are a lot of options.

Even if you "just want a steak", it is easy to pick the wrong one. If you shop at the supermarket, you may not find these 5 particular steaks. How will you know which steak to pick? How often do you stare at the cuts and the price, unsure of which piece of meat to buy?

Here's how you use the meat chart. The cow stands on four legs and does not lie down too often. The working muscles in the neck, shoulders and legs contain lots of fibers and connective tissue. These muscles get a lot of exercise and are tough because of it. The best way to tenderize these cuts is long, slow cooking using moist heat, like braising or stewing.

So if you buy a Chuck Steak from the supermarket and cook it using dry heat, like grilling or pan frying, because it is labeled as a steak, you probably won't be happy with the results. It may have good flavor, but it will be tough to chew. If you know that the Chuck is located in the shoulder, you know that Chuck Steak is better for stew! You won't be fooled again!

Another cut that is confusing is London Broil. Actually there is no such cut of meat. London Broil is a method of preparation. It describes a way to cook steak medium and slice it. The problem is that you have purchased a mystery cut of meat. Hopefully it is from the sirloin and it will be nice and tender when you cook it in this manner.

A Word of Warning: Beware the Eye of the Round! The eye of the round looks like a small beef tenderloin. It's cylindrical and there's no fat on it. The difference is the eye of the round is a working muscle and the tenderloin is not. If you cook the eye of the round at high heat to rare or medium rare, it will be good value for the money. **But if you like your meat well done, you (and everyone else) are going to think you don't know how to cook, because the Eye of the Round will be virtually inedible.**

It's NOT your fault! This is about marketing. Think about it. Have you ever seen the eye of the round on a restaurant menu? This is a supermarket cut of meat sold to unsuspecting home cooks. To me, it's criminal. This is why I strongly believe, if you know how to shop, cooking becomes so much easier. You have to buy the right ingredient to get the proper result.

You should have a credit card sized laminated Meat Chart in your wallet whenever you go to the supermarket. I'm totally serious. **At least be aware of where the best cuts are, if you are shopping for a steak, and what to do with the less expensive cuts.**

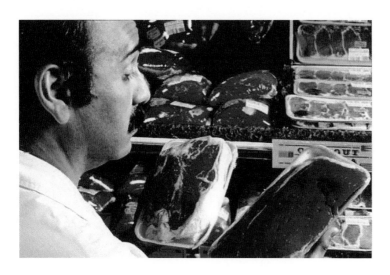

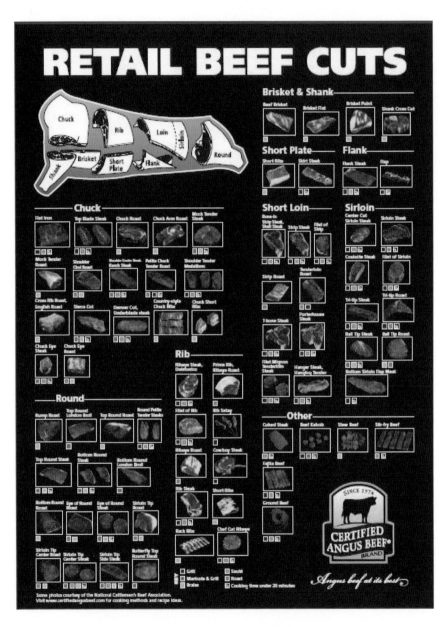

Reprinted Courtesy of the National Cattleman's Beef Association

CHAPTER 8

"Life expectancy would grow by leaps and bounds if green vegetables smelled as good as bacon."
Doug Larson

At one time, pork used to be very fatty. So much so, that you could cook it with dry or moist heat and the cut would "self-baste" from the melting fat. The pork industry changed that through genetic engineering, diet and butchering techniques. Now, lean cuts of pork are readily available.

This creates a problem for the home cook. On one hand, lean meat is better for you, but means there is less fat. If you cook meat well done that does not have fat, it dries out and becomes tough. As I stated earlier, with fat comes flavor, and pork fat is the best. **Lastly, there is a fear of trichinosis in this country, which is present in under cooked pork. I cook pork medium well because the flavor and texture improve dramatically and cases of trichinosis are rare in the US. The choice is yours.**

The anatomy of a pig is much less complicated than a cow, when it comes to identifying cuts to cook. Most of the pig (the legs) is cured as ham, and cooked by moist heat methods. Spareribs and bacon come from the belly and the lean cuts come from the loin which extends along the back, from the shoulder to the rump. The loin cuts are cooked using dry heat methods. The only confusing cut is the Boston Butt which is located in the shoulder, not in the rump.

"Down South, even our vegetables have some pig hidden somewhere in it. A vegetable isn't a vegetable without a little ham hock"
Paula Deen

CHAPTER 9

"Is this chicken, what I have, or is this fish? I know it's tuna, but it says Chicken of the Sea."
Jessica Simpson

I started eating fish as a child, so it has always been a part of my diet. I have also lived close to the ocean, all my life. So fish and seafood are common cooking ingredients in my home. This isn't the case for everyone. Maybe you like fish, and maybe you don't. Fish is different from the other animals we eat for several reasons.

Most people don't hunt their own beef, pork or chicken in the wild, then bring it home dress it and eat it. Perhaps it is because they are not mammals and we don't really understand what goes on "under the sea". Are you aware that less than 5% of imported seafood is inspected? **But, it may not surprise you that the most commonly prepared fish in US households is canned tuna.** Maybe it is because it doesn't taste like fish…

Yet there is an incredible variety of seafood available in most supermarkets. In south Florida, it is even common to find a sushi station next to the seafood counter. Fish does contain high levels of protein and most fish is very lean compared to other meat.

I suggest buying seafood from a fishmonger for the same reason as I suggested buying meat from a butcher. It is their specialty and they can help educate you on the most appropriate choice for your meal. Because seafood generally freezes well, you may find a selection of seafood in your supermarket freezer section.

It is much easier to judge the quality of a whole fish. Unfortunately, most supermarkets don't carry them. The eyes should be clear and bulging, not sunken. The gills should be intact and red. The scales should be firmly affixed and transparent and the body should be firm to the touch. And it should not smell "off", even in the body cavity.

Most of the fish you will encounter will be in fillets or steaks. The two fillets are cut from either side of the fish from behind the gills, along the backbone, to the tail. Often there are a few (rib) bones still present in a fillet of fish. You should be asked if you want them removed. Fish steaks are cut like a cross-section of the fish right through the backbone. It will certainly have bones, so make sure you (and your guests) are aware of that.

There are so many different kinds of fish available, that it is beyond the scope of this book to explain the best method of preparation for each. It should be noted that most fish begins to flake when it is cooked and becomes very delicate, making it difficult to keep intact. Be sure to go to http://ChefMartyRich.com/book-bonus/ and receive your ***Secret Ingredients to Successful Cooking.***

"If you give a person a fish, they'll fish for a day. But if you train a person to fish, they'll fish for a lifetime." Dan Quayle

Chapter 10

"It takes a tough man to make a tender chicken."
Frank Perdue

Chicken is the perfect flavor palate to use when you are interested in experimenting with seasonings. It does not have a strong flavor and the texture is very good, unless you overcook it. **Chicken is also easily adaptable to most methods of preparation, giving you the opportunity to be creative with an inexpensive main course.**

There are choices in most supermarkets with respect to quality. There is a significant price increase when you purchase organic or free range chicken. It is your choice whether or not it is worth it, but I believe you can tell the difference. It is easy to get confused by the labels.

Another interesting fact I learned as a butcher is the difference between "fresh" and "frozen". According to the USDA, fresh means whole poultry and cuts have never been below 26 °F, while frozen poultry is kept 0 °F or below. Why does that matter? The upside is that chicken does freeze well, but the downside is you should buy it frozen if you are going to freeze it later. Chicken does not store well at refrigerated temperatures. Plan to cook it within a couple of days of purchase.

It is also more economical to buy a whole chicken and cut it up yourself, unless everyone likes white meat or dark meat. You pay a premium price for boneless, skinless chicken breast. Cutting a chicken into 8 pieces will take you less than 5 minutes with just a little practice.

"Left wing, chicken wing, it don't make no difference to me." Woody Guthrie

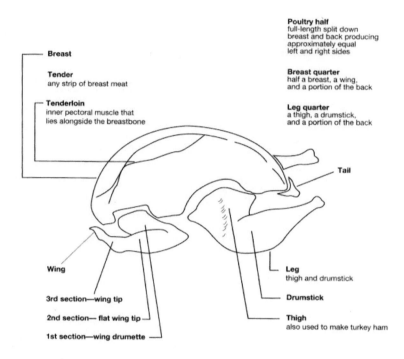

Breast

Tender
any strip of breast meat

Tenderloin
inner pectoral muscle that
lies alongside the breastbone

Poultry half
full-length split down
breast and back producing
approximately equal
left and right sides

Breast quarter
half a breast, a wing,
and a portion of the back

Leg quarter
a thigh, a drumstick,
and a portion of the back

Tail

Wing

3rd section—wing tip

2nd section— flat wing tip

1st section—wing drumette

Leg
thigh and drumstick

Drumstick

Thigh
also used to make turkey ham

Much like pork, chicken is closely associated with foodborne illness. **Salmonella is found in chicken, but is killed at temperatures required for chicken to be completely cooked (165°F). The best way to ensure that it is cooked properly is to use a meat thermometer**. Measure the temperature in several places if you are roasting a whole chicken.

The other reason to use a meat thermometer is that you don't want to overcook the chicken. It will become dry quickly after the internal temperature rises above 170 degrees. **After the chicken is finished cooking, let it rest for a 5 to 10 minutes before you cut into the chicken and serve. This will help to keep the juices inside the bird, rather than on your cutting board. The same is true for meat.**

CHAPTER 11

An onion can make people cry but there's never been a vegetable that can make people laugh.   Will Rogers

A wider variety of fruits and vegetables are available now, than ever before. Most of us have a habit of eating what we have always eaten, and when we shop, we don't even see many of the choices we have. With produce being flown in from every corner of the earth, it is possible to try new foods whenever the mood strikes. Not only are supermarkets providing seasonal produce, they are catering to the ethnic diversity of their customers.

Produce is cheap enough to try new things. You may discover something new you enjoy! If I find a new fruit or vegetable that looks interesting, I ask the produce manager about it. Often I just buy it, then "Google It" to find a recipe. Most vegetables are not complicated to prepare. Most can be simply steamed, pan fried, or roasted until soft, then seasoned and eaten.

How many of these fruits and vegetables can you name?

So how do you pick a good one? Don't be afraid to pick them up, feel them, and smell them. They should be firm to the touch. Look for bruises and blemishes. Obviously, avoid any produce that is moldy or has signs of insect damage. Check to see if the color is consistent from end to end. **Smell the fruit. It may look a little strange, but if a pineapple doesn't smell sweet…it's not. A peach should smell like a peach and a tomato should smell like a tomato.**

Be sure to keep your produce separate from your meat and poultry in the shopping cart. Put the raw meat in plastic bags to ensure your produce is not contaminated by pathogens in the blood. Also, be sure to keep cleaning products separate as well.

I keep my eye on the produce when I'm checking out too. After you have carefully selected your fruits and vegetables, don't let the checker or the bagger toss your food around. Make sure the easily bruised fruit is on top, rather than packed in on the bottom next to the carrots or apples. It takes a little more effort, but it is worth it!

Refrigeration can prevent some produce from ripening. For example, tomatoes ripen to a better tomato flavor, a softer texture, and red color if they are left at room temperature. In the refrigerator, they will remain firm, they do not turn red, and even red tomatoes kept in the refrigerator lose their flavor.

Certain fruits and vegetables should not be stored together. Apples, avocados, bananas, melons, tomatoes, peaches, pears, passion fruit and papayas all produce ethylene gas that adversely affect some other vegetables. Ethylene sensitive vegetables include Iceberg, broccoli, carrots, cucumbers, parsley and leafy greens. Onions cause potatoes to spoil much faster, so try to keep them separated as well.

If you don't have the space to keep all your produce segregated, just be aware of the situation and try to use the fruits and vegetables you buy in 3 to 5 days. If you buy vegetables with leafy tops like carrots, beets, fennel, etc…cut them off. Nutrients will continue to flow from the veggie to the stems, as long as they remain attached

Do not wash vegetables until you are ready to use them. If you do wash them ahead, be sure to dry them completely. The excess moisture will cause them to spoil faster. All produce, (save onions) should be washed, even if you are going to peel them. A salad spinner is particularly useful if you eat a lot of leafy greens.

If a particular vegetable or fruit is not available, don't overlook the freezer section. It's the next best thing to fresh. **Frozen vegetables are usually picked at their peak, and then processed. Fresh produce is usually picked before it is ripe, so it can be shipped more efficiently and has an extended shelf life.** The exception is produce found at a farmer's market. Because the time and distance is short from field to market, local farmers can sell produce at its peak of ripeness.

"Go vegetable heavy. Reverse the psychology of your plate by making meat the side dish and vegetables the main course." Bobby Flay

STEAK TIP

I am not suggesting which is better for you. When I have easy access to it and I can afford it, I buy organic. Although it is more available now than ever, it can still be hard to find and the selection is usually small outside of metro areas. The American Cancer Society (ACS) has said "whether organic foods carry a lower risk of cancer because they are less likely to be contaminated by compounds that might cause cancer is largely unknown" but "vegetables, fruits, and whole grains should form the central part of a person's diet, regardless of whether they are grown conventionally or organically".

The Environmental Working Group publishes a list of "The Dirty Dozen" and "The Clean 15" each year based on data from the US Department of Agriculture and the US Food and Drug Administration. For more information, go to their website, www.FoodNews.org. You can find these lists on the next page.

I hope I have impressed upon you why shopping is so important when it comes to ingredients. The more you know about the raw ingredients, the better your cooked food will be. There is a lot to know and I have barely skimmed the surface. Take your time. You have a lifetime of trial and error to understand food and cooking.

Remember that a supermarket is constructed to separate you from your money. So much research goes into the layout of a grocery store. Every one of the 35,000 items is strategically placed for optimum sales, whether at the end of the aisle, or at checkout, eye level, or the "fresh" products line the walls vs. the processed foods in the isles. It's easy to get distracted.

Make sure you're getting value for your money and not empty calories and over processed food. I'm not being critical of supermarkets as much as I want to impress upon you how to be selective when you shop so that you are much more successful in the kitchen.

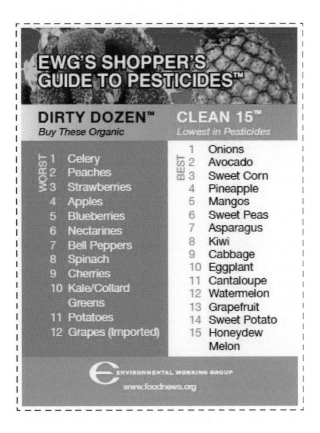

"Researchers in the U.K. have developed a vegetable called super broccoli designed to fight heart disease. Not to be outdone, researchers in America have developed a way to stuff an Oreo inside another Oreo."
Jimmy Fallon

NOTES

CHAPTER 12

"You learn to cook so that you don't have to be a slave to recipes. You get what's in season and you know what to do with it."   Julia Child

Timothy Ferriss stated that there were two principles that applied to all learning. The first was failure points, and the second was the margin of safety. His margin of safety with regards to cooking is "bullet-proof recipes". My first thought was, how can a beginner cook find good recipes?

I guess I did not understand what he meant. His margin of safety was not about finding good recipes, it was: "How badly can you mangle the recipe and still get something incredible?" Then he restated it this way: "You guarantee a good meal by picking the recipes well, not by following recipes well."

WHAT?!? I read it several times and I still don't comprehend what he is trying to say. I'm not going to put words into his mouth, trying to guess what he is saying. I am going to explain why I think you should learn to cook before you begin using recipes.

Start by choosing the best ingredients you can find. You should already know how to pick quality ingredients based on the information in the previous chapters. Let's just pick chicken for this example. If you are not ready to cut a whole chicken into pieces, then buy your favorite part(s) pre-cut.

Then choose a method of preparation. I will describe many different methods of preparation in Chapter 15, but for now, let's

59

use the oven. Pre-heat the oven to 350°F. Season the chicken simply with salt and pepper. Then put the chicken pieces on a baking sheet and cook until done. **Finally, you know it's done when a meat thermometer registers the internal temp at 165°F.**

Bon Appetite!

Next time, pick a different method of preparation, but keep it just as simple. When you feel comfortable cooking chicken several different ways, then try cooking fish, or steak, or a vegetable. Just focus on one ingredient at a time and notice how the taste changes with the method. Also note how the time it takes to cook changes with each method used to cook it. **This is learning how to cook. Be sure to go to http://ChefMartyRich.com/book-bonus/ and receive your Secret Ingredients to Successful Cooking**

Begin cooking just once or twice a week. If you start with a boneless breast of chicken, move to bone-in chicken breast, a half chicken, and a whole chicken. You will be surprised at how much variety you can get from just one ingredient. When you learn to grill, roast, braise, and fry, you will be able to eat chicken for months without preparing the same dish twice. **This is learning how to cook.**

Once you understand how to cook, recipes will be much easier to follow because you have mastered the basics. Recipes add a depth of flavor to the simple dishes you already know how to prepare. Each step in a recipe should add another layer of flavor until the finished dish is much more than the sum of its parts.

The problem with learning from cookbooks is that all recipes are not created equal. **Every cookbook is written for a different audience and a different purpose.** You may find some recipes in a beginner's cookbook too challenging. Even if you follow the basic rules for choosing a recipe, outlined above, there is no guarantee of success. I agree with Mr. Ferriss on this point.

A recipe is really a chemical equation, and often the instructions are open to interpretation. If someone gives you a recipe, they usually have a few tips or clarifications to help you make it properly. Apparently, some of these details were left out, at least according to the person who shared the recipe with you.

"Even though I'm big on recipes, I love to make up my own dishes and when you take a risk in the kitchen, you learn a lot about food!"
Nina Dobrev

NOTES

CHAPTER 13

"Recipes are important but only to a point. What's more important than recipes is how we think about food, and a good cookbook should open up a new way of doing just that." Michael Symon

So if cookbooks can't be trusted, where do you start? I'm going to suggest a couple of cooking magazines, "Cook's Illustrated" and "Fine Cooking". After you have mastered the basics and you want to take your cooking to the next level, these resources will take you there. These magazines focus exclusively on food and cooking. They examine seasonal ingredients, explore methods of preparation and evaluate kitchen tools and equipment.

Cook's Illustrated is self-described as "America's Test Kitchen". "Our mission is to test recipes over and over again until we understand how and why they work and until we arrive at the best version. We also test kitchen equipment and supermarket ingredients in search of brands that offer the best value and performance."

Every one of the recipes has been tested multiple times, which is the best margin of safety. The beauty of their format is they explain what happened during the testing phase and reveal comments made by the tasters. The experimentation and ingredient research is done for you! You will not find a better cooking class.

When they explain it this way, you understand how each ingredient affects the finished product. So, if you like your macaroni and cheese really rich, you might use heavy cream. If you want your mac and cheese to have fewer calories, you might want to use skim milk. That's why I love the magazine. It's cover to cover cooking. There are no advertisements or articles about travel or fashion.

The other magazine I really enjoy is Fine Cooking. Fine Cooking is a high glossy, full color magazine while Cook's Illustrated is primarily printed in black and white. So if you are into "food porn", Fine Cooking is for you. Sometimes it's all in the presentation. I get both magazines because they are educational, and I believe the recipes are consistently better than most of the cookbooks I own.

Fine Cooking is full of information and training for a home cook. There are advertisements, but they are all food related. The food photography will make you drool, so if that is what excites you, then try Fine Cooking. **If you really love food photography, check out http://foodporndaily.com.** It is up close and personal. Rated G.

These two magazines, in combination, are the most appropriate follow up to this book I could suggest. With tested recipes, a focus on seasonal ingredients, instruction on correct technique, and equipment and product reviews, you get a well-rounded education for $6 or $7 dollars per issue.

Even if you only cook a couple of times a week, you should make an effort to prepare several dishes from both magazines. There's a wide variety of menus from soups and side dishes, to salads, appetizers, sauces, main dishes, meatless meals and desserts. Cook's Illustrated is published every month and Fine Cooking is published every other month.

"I was eating in a Chinese restaurant downtown. There was a dish called Mother and Child Reunion. It's chicken and eggs. And I said, I gotta use that one." Paul Simon

I have a cookbook collection with close to 400 titles. So I am not suggesting that you never buy cookbooks. There was a time that I would love nothing better than to thumb through a new cookbook, but I have packed all my cookbooks away and relegated them to the storage unit. Now, I just Google a recipe and in less than a second, I have access to more recipes than I care to read.

I read through four or five or six, and I come up with the one that sounds best to me or takes the least amount of time or lists the ingredients that I have on hand or the method of preparation that works best for me, and I print out the recipe and I'm off to the races. If I want to see some pictures of presentations, I just click on "Images" and I get pages of pictures in another second.

How do you know if a cookbook is any good? Pick two or three recipes and follow them. If you like the results, it's time to buy. If the steps are confusing or you don't like the results, save your money. You may have to kiss a bunch of frogs before you find a cookbook that is full of "bullet-proof" recipes.

Everyone cooks differently. Everyone has their own style. It is very difficult to replicate a recipe, even your own recipe, consistently. To me, every meal is a creative and unique adventure and I use what's on hand to make the best dishes I can. **The beautiful thing is, you don't have to find your style…it finds you.**

I would like to illustrate my point with an interesting story about a cooking class I attended in Bali. The class was held at a beautiful resort, right on the ocean, and there were eleven of us taking this Indonesian cooking class. It was the first day of class and we were standing around this great big table with the chef standing at the head of the table.

Each of us had our own little cooking station with a portable burner, a wok, several containers of identically prepped ingredients, and a recipe for fried rice. The chef gathered us around and demonstrated the dish first, walking us through the recipe, step-by-step. Everyone was watching closely as each ingredient was added to the wok according to the recipe, until the dish was complete.

Then, it was our turn to make fried rice. The chef was there answering our questions as we went along. After everyone was done cooking their fried rice, twelve spoons were placed at each station, and we were invited to go around the table and taste everyone's fried rice. No two fried rice dishes tasted the same! It was absolutely amazing to all of us. Even using the same recipe, the same ingredients, and the same cooking equipment, our food reflected our own style.

So share your recipes! No one cooks like you. It does not make it good or bad…just different. It's about the journey, not the destination. Enjoy the process. I love being as excited as anyone else at the table when my meal is REALLY good! Enjoy every time you make something. It may never come out the same again. You might never know that little thing that you did last time that you forgot to do this time. This is where I find the joy in cooking.

Not only do we cook differently, but we also have a unique sense of taste and food preferences. Do you like your vegetables cooked crunchy or soft? Do you like your potatoes boiled with the skin on or off? Do you like your meat or rare or medium or well-done? Do you like sushi or your fish cooked, or does the smell of seafood make you nauseous? Try to be considerate of those you are serving and their tastes as well. They will be happy you took the time and effort.

It is not always easy to adapt a recipe to your taste. I always suggest you follow the recipe the first time you make it. Our neighbor and I have a running feud over this. She has an "aversion" to following the recipe, as written, even the first time. If it does not come out the way she expected, then how will she identify the problem? This is especially true when it comes to baking.

Cooking and baking are completely different "sports"! There are many chefs who do not bake and bakers who do not cook. When you are cooking, you can change ingredients and seasonings as you go along. In fact, right up to bringing the food to the table, you can continue to "manipulate" the flavor of the finished dish.

In baking, most of the work is done before the dish goes into the oven. In fact, baking recipes are called formulas, because each ingredient should be weighed to ensure consistent results. It's a controlled chemical reaction.

To get back to my point, whether it's your particular taste or that of your guests, it's important to plan ahead. For example, if I like my meat medium rare and someone else prefers well done, I have to cook two different pieces of meat, so we can both enjoy the same meal. In entertaining, it's good to know what the tastes of your guests are. Knowing their preferences ahead of time will make your meal preparation go much smoother.

Each restaurant has a particular style and atmosphere that makes the establishment special. Guests come in to enjoy their style. Many restaurants don't go too far out of their way to accommodate you, if you don't like their style. Good luck getting a vegan plate in a steak house.

When I became a private chef, everything changed. My cooking now reflects my guest's style. My goal is to accommodate someone else's tastes. It's a subtle, but significant difference. **Try cooking to please others, rather than cooking to please yourself. I think you will be pleasantly surprised with the result...and so will they.**

Be sure to go to http://ChefMartyRich.com/book-bonus/ and receive your *Secret Ingredients to Successful Cooking*

"**One of the things that often frustrates me with cookbooks is that there are one or two recipes that are really good and the rest of them are not so great.**"
Alicia Silverstone

CHAPTER 14

"Getting into the habit of switching a timer on will, I promise, save you from any number of kitchen disasters." Delia Smith

"I don't have time to cook." Sound familiar? Is it that you don't have time to cook, or that you don't have time to continue making mistakes in the kitchen? **I believe you would make time for cooking if you were better at it.**

I am not going to try to convince you that home cooked food is quicker than fast food. But if you are going to order takeout from home, wait for them to cook it, go pick it up, then bring it home and sit down for dinner, it will probably take more than 30 minutes. There are a lot of meals you can make in 30 minutes or less.

I realize that you have to include shopping and cleanup when you discuss the time it takes to cook. But if you "share the load", then cooking does not have to dominate your day. The combination of all these chores is what I mean by the "time" it takes to cook. "Timing", with regards to cooking is slightly different.

A common frustration that happens to all of us on occasion is, not getting the food ready at the same time. There are several ways to eliminate this problem including advanced planning, knowing your ingredients, and using your kitchen timer. This is what I mean by "timing".

Time and timing are closely related. I will give you an example to illustrate. I am going to cook a simple, Sunday dinner tonight. We will have roast chicken, potatoes, corn, broccoli, and a garden salad. I'm going to figure it will take about an hour from when I walk into the kitchen, until it's on the table.

How do I figure that out? Know your ingredients. I'm roasting a whole chicken and I know it takes about an hour. (Remember learning the basics?) If I cut the chicken in half, I can save about 10 to 15 minutes cooking time. Once the chicken is in the oven, I won't have to watch it at all until I take its temperature. (Chicken should be cooked to an internal temperature of 165°F.)

If you are following a recipe, it will always give you an idea of how long it will take to complete the dish. The chicken is going to take longer than any other item on the menu. The exception is if we are having baked potatoes, which can take an hour or more depending on their size. My point is that once you determine which dish is going to take the longest to finish, you have established the "time" before the meal is complete. I give myself an extra 10 or 15 minutes more time than the longest cooking dish, just in case.

Let's look more closely at Sunday dinner. I start by preheating the oven. I always start by getting my cooking source ready first. Then I split the chicken and season both sides with salt and pepper. You can add any other seasoning from your pantry that you like. I use aluminum foil on my sheet pan. I realize it's not the most earth friendly thing to do, but it sure as heck makes clean-up easier. It's for you to decide.

I pop the seasoned chicken into my preheated oven. I like cooking at higher temperatures (400°F or 425°F). The chicken will cook faster, but it will shrink more as well. Once the chicken is in the oven, I can just move on to the next dish. The starch is usually the next longest cooking item. Most dried pastas need to boil for 10 – 12 minutes and white rice needs to simmer for 20. If you prefer brown rice and it takes 45 minutes or more, then start the rice first, and then the chicken. In this case, we are having potatoes.

We are having roasted potatoes tonight. I have red bliss potatoes and all I have to do is put them on the same tray as the chicken. If they are large, I will cut them in half or quarters. If they are small, I will roast them whole. That was fast! What is left?

I should still have 20 minutes or more left before the chicken is done. Either frozen corn or fresh corn on the cob will only take 5 to 7 minutes, if the water is already hot. Steamed broccoli will be cooked in about the same amount of time. Once the pans have water and the heat is on, it's time to make the salad. When it gets within 10 minutes of "show time", I'm checking each dish closely to see if it is done…especially those in the oven that I can't see.

Admittedly, things can get hectic when everything is done at the same time. Now you have the opposite problem! Just know that the chicken can sit outside of the oven for 10 minutes without getting cold. The same is true for a pot of rice or pasta. **Don't panic! One helpful tip is to have serving bowls and utensils out and ready**

for each dish that is finished cooking. Serve family style.

If you began cooking just one dish at a time, as I suggested, then each step should be easy for you. There is a method to my madness! When I taught myself to juggle, I started with three balls and I couldn't get the rhythm until I started with just one ball. When it became second nature to toss the ball up with one hand and catch it with the other, I added the second ball.

Then I juggled two balls and learned how to keep my attention on both simultaneously. You have to know when to release the first ball before you can catch the second. It's the same with cooking. You have to keep your eye on two dishes, and when you pay too much attention to one, the second dish burns.

When it came to juggling three balls, my breakthrough came when I stopped panicking. You have to relax and let each ball rise to its peak before throwing the next. When you have three dishes going at the same time, you have to constantly monitor when each will be done cooking and continually make adjustments. That's why Thanksgiving is such a big event for a home cook. You could have 8 or more dishes to get on the table at the same time.

Are you making beef stew using chuck? It's going to take an hour and a half before that meat becomes tender. You can't put your carrots and potatoes in the stew at the beginning with the meat unless you like really mushy vegetables. Simply apply the lessons learned when mastering the ingredients and add a timer. You will be less confused about timing and you meals will be better coordinated.

Ultimately, you control the timing of your dishes by the way you prepare the ingredients and by how you like your food cooked. That is why I have mentioned quality ingredients and methods of preparation over and over again. Rachel Ray has a popular cooking show entitled "30 Minute Meals". You can do it too, if you cook chicken cutlets instead of bone-in chicken breasts, or boiled potatoes instead of oven baked potatoes. If a dish is cooking a little too fast, turn it down or shut it off. If it's done cooking way ahead of time, just set it on the side and hopefully it will stay warm until you are ready or you can try to reheat it at the last minute. Eventually you will learn how long it takes to cook various ingredients and your timing will improve. You have to practice.

We have a rule in our house which is I cook you clean, you cook I clean. This is another stress reliever. Share the load. After you have put the meal together, gotten it on the table and everyone's eaten...the kitchen sink is piled with dirty pots and pans. How about a little help? When the shopping, cooking, and clean-up are the responsibility of one person, it can be daunting.

If you can convince someone else in your household to learn how to cook with you, it will increase the probability that you will stick with it. They enjoy their day of cooking without having to do the dishes and vice versa. The other person gets to just sit down for diner, in exchange for loading the dishwasher. It's a pretty good deal, if you can get someone else to help.

When I Said "I Do" I Didn't' Mean the Dishes

CHAPTER 14

"In department stores, so much kitchen equipment is bought indiscriminately by people who just come in for men's underwear." Julia Child

There are a lot of ways to go about preparing your kitchen for cooking. The method Timothy Ferriss suggested was as he introduced recipes, he included a shopping list of food ingredients and equipment purchases to be made. Over the course of preparing these recipes, you would learn methods of cooking and acquire necessary pieces of equipment to outfit your kitchen.

I think a little different. You should use whatever you have. I go back to my college days when we only had a grill. We cooked an amazing array of food on that grill. Maybe you inherited a mismatched collection of tools, pots and pans. That's fine. It's better to get started and upgrade as you go, than buy equipment for a recipe and never use it again.

My parents' house is a one bedroom log cabin with a teeny, tiny kitchen. It is 7 feet square. It's small, with very little counter space. They have an electric stove and oven, a microwave, a two bay sink, and a refrigerator/freezer. They have no food processor or blender or Kitchen Aid Stand Mixer. The silverware drawer and the miscellaneous/tools drawer are so jammed with stuff, that they are hard to open. Yet, I have made Thanksgiving Dinner for 12 in that little tiny kitchen.

These are our kitchen drawers. I suggest you use what you've got. No excuses.

Your cooking will improve when you start to upgrade your equipment. The handles come loose from a cheap pot. It won't sit flat on the burner after a while because the bottom warps. Because it is warped, your food does not cook evenly and there is a much greater chance that you will burn your food. They are also harder to clean, so when you break out a steel wool pad to clean the burnt food, the finish usually comes off too. You don't want to eat that!

If you are just getting started, you only need a 2 qt. saucepan, a 10 inch sauté pan and an 8 qt. stockpot with covers. You will have to be more organized with just 3 pans, but you will find it doesn't take many more. The more pots and pans you have, the more you will dirty! I make Thanksgiving Dinner with 4 pots, (1, 2, 4, and 8 qt.), 2 frying pans (7 in. non-stick, and 10 in.) and a roasting pan for the turkey (that fits your oven).

It's great to have food processors, blenders, juicers, this and that. Well, yes and no… It really depends how interested you get in cooking. As your interest grows, your desire/need/want for better equipment will probably go up. At this point, you will probably follow Mr. Ferriss' advice and purchase tools in order to make recipes you find interesting.

"The best thing I have is the knife from Fatal Attraction. I hung it in my kitchen. It's my way of saying, Don't mess with me." Glenn Close

If you've got one of those old hand me down knives, but you like it, use it. **I am NOT going to suggest that you go out and buy a $200 professional blade.** I own a whole bunch of expensive knives, but I use their simple Ginsu-like, always sharp, knife set. A sharp knife is a sharp knife and a dull knife is a dull knife at the end of the day. It's preferable to have a sharp knife in case you're wondering.

Go with what works for you. When I watch some people grab a knife to cut some veggies, chills go up and down my spine. I can't believe they don't cut themselves. But you have to do what's comfortable for you. Far be it for me to come in and say, "No, no, no, that's not how you hold a knife. No, no, no, that's not how you cut an onion." That's silly. If you want to learn the "proper way", I will provide links to some YouTube training videos in the resource section.

I hope you never get the feeling that you're doing it the "wrong way". If you don't know how to do it, then yes, you can be taught. **If you use a knife every day without cutting yourself, stick with it.** I want to eliminate the barriers (real or perceived) that are keeping you from culinary confidence.

If you have nothing, then I would definitely start out with an <u>8 inch Victorinox Chef knife</u>. It's very simple knife that's used in a lot of restaurants. It's not one of the high end knives, but it will probably keep an edge longer than an expensive knife. It's $30. Many people suggest buying a paring knife as well, for small jobs. I just use a steak knife from the drawer.

If I bought a second knife, I would buy a serrated bread knife. Make sure you buy a cutting board, if you don't have one. It will protect your knife and your counters.

"I probably use my chef's knives more than any other tool in the kitchen. I'm not married to a particular brand, because they all work, they all have sharp blades."
Bobby Flay

The essential tools that you saw in our kitchen drawer on the right are tongs, a peeler, wooden spoons, a potato masher, a slotted spoon, a box grater, a whetstone, the meat thermometer, and a good can opener. The other tools I put in that category are sturdy sheet pans, a colander, a cutting board, and wire racks.

The rest of my kitchen utensils are for baking. A whisk, a rubber spatula, measuring cups and spoons, and a set of stainless mixing bowls are about all you need to get started. You also need an assortment of baking tins including an 8 inch square, a 9x5 loaf pan, a 9x13 casserole dish, a couple of 9 inch cake pans, a 12 cup muffin tin, and a sturdy jelly roll sheet pan.

After saying "just start with what you have", my essential tool list grew pretty fast! **The bottom-line is to buy each item when you become committed to using it and when you can afford it.** All of the tools, including the pots and pans listed on the previous page can cost you less than $300.

"I am spoiled, it's true. I don't even know how to use that thing in the kitchen with the burners." Cindy Margolis

Chef Marty Rich

NOTES

CHAPTER 16

Everything in food is science. The only subjective part is when you eat it.   Alton Brown

I have used the term "method of preparation" over and over again. I'm sure you know it simply means different ways to cook your food. There's a number of different ways to prepare your food depending upon the ingredient, how fast you want to cook it, your dietary concerns, what you like to eat, the kitchen you are cooking in, the season, the equipment you have, etc...

Mastering these techniques will come with practice. If you start by focusing on one quality ingredient and learn how to cook it a few different ways, you will make progress quickly. Most recipes assume that you know at least this much about cooking. I know it seems elementary...even "pre-school" if you already learned the hard way. **Share this book with someone who is just starting.**

Which source of heat is better, electric or gas? Whatever! Just use what you have. You'll get used to using whichever one you have. Electric burners take longer to heat and cool, but electric ovens provide more even heat. Once you learn the quirks of your equipment, you will fall in love with it...warts and all.

It is more important to make sure your oven is calibrated properly, than to worry about the type of heat. Get an oven thermometer to check it. I'm not an appliance repairman, and I don't play one on TV, so I don't know how to calibrate your oven, but at least you will know how many degrees it is off and make the proper adjustment when you use it.

As far as we know, grilling is the oldest cooking technique. So let's begin with grilling and broiling. Whether you use gas or electric, the distinction between them is based on where the heat is coming from. In grilling, the heat source is from the bottom, and in broiling, it is from the top. In either case, the heat is only coming from one direction. You control the intensity of the heat using the temperature knob, and changing the distance between the food and the heat source.

The purpose of either technique is to brown or give a crust to the food. Because of the intensity of the heat, the thickness of the food matters. If the food is too thick, and the heat too high, the outside burns before the inside is cooked. If the food is thicker than an inch or two, you can move it further from the heat source. You can cook a turkey on an outdoor grill if you move it away from the direct heat.

In the dry heat methods, the food is cooked by the heat drying out the food. The more intense the heat source, the quicker it dries. If the food does not contain fat (boneless chicken breasts) to self-baste, the food can get too dry and overcook very fast. That's what condiments are for...

Keep your eye on your food with either method. If you are grilling, dripping fat can create flare ups and fire. Flames are not your friend. Once your food catches on fire, it is tough to save. If you're broiling a dish in the oven, your food is out of sight and out of mind. Stay vigilant or use a timer!

If you are not using a timer, I suggest you lower the rack to the middle shelf or lower, if you broil on "HIGH". Once your dish starts burning, the presentation (and taste) will suffer. You may be able to save the dish by removing the burnt crust and browning again. **It's better to take a little longer for your food to brown, than to have to reset the smoke alarm or call for takeout.**

"I updated my grilling app, iGrill, today and it now has Facebook integration that lets you see what other people are grilling right now around the world. Awesome."
Mark Zuckerberg

Roasting and baking are also considered dry heat methods of cooking, but unlike grilling or broiling, the heat is indirect. Roasting is usually done at higher temperatures (over 400 degrees), and baking more commonly refers to bread, cakes and pastry and is cooked at lower temperatures.

Roasting at high temperatures will brown the food. When food is browned, it means that the natural sugars are caramelizing and this creates depth of flavor to the dish. The juices that escape and the bits that stick to the pan can be used to flavor a jus, sauce, or gravy.

When roasting or baking, make sure that you preheat your oven. I've already written about this, but it deserves repeating. When you are about to cook any food, you must remember to prepare the heat source first. If you don't, chances are you will have the food ready for the oven, and the oven won't be ready for the food. Unless you're making yeast leavened bread that will take hours to rise, the first step of almost every other baking recipe is "Preheat the oven to…"

"Man who waits for roast duck to fly into mouth must wait very, very long time." Jules Renard

Sautér in French means "to jump." When you put wet food into hot oil, you will understand what it means "to jump"! Oil will splatter everywhere. Cooking food in even a small amount of hot oil will create a crust and keep the food from sticking to the pan.

Although it is not intuitive, sautéing is also a dry heat method. The hot oil seals the moisture inside the food and the food steams in its own juices from the inside. When the moisture escapes and makes contact with the hot oil, you hear the snap, crackle and pop. Be careful, it's easy to get burned.

Preheat the empty pan first. Just how hot the pan should be depends on the type of oil you are cooking with. There will be trial and error with this process. **If the pan is too hot, the oil will immediately begin to smoke. This is known as its smoke point.** This is the temperature when the oil begins to breakdown. Each type of oil has a different smoke point. Butter has a very low smoke point because it has milk solids in it that burn easily. Canola or vegetable oil has a higher smoke point.

If the oil is too hot and it's really smoking, don't use it. You will burn your food to a crisp in a matter of seconds. Also be aware that extremely hot oil can be flammable. If the oil does catch fire, put a cover on it to smother the flame. **DO NOT ADD WATER TO**

THE PAN!!!

While the pan can be too hot, it can be too cold to fry. If you do not properly preheat the pan, your food will not brown and the coating will absorb the oil rather than making a crust. Preheat the empty pan for a minute or more. Place your hand 2 or 3 inches from the surface of the pan to check that there is heat radiating from it. Pour in enough oil to coat the bottom of the pan. The oil should begin to shimmer before you add the food.

Make sure you do not crowd the pan with the food. The oil must remain hot and if too much moisture escapes from the food, it will steam, not fry. Saute several small batches rather than squeezing in all the food at one time. Place the fried items on a plate covered with paper towels to absorb excess oil and keep warm in a low temperature oven if possible.

To serve a sauce with the sautéed food, pour off the remaining oil when you are finished sautéing. The crusty bits that are stuck to the pan will add flavor to your sauce. You can add stock, wine, cream and/or citrus juice to the pan to loosen those bits. Reduce the liquid to thicken slightly and pour over the sautéed food.

**"The food in Europe is pretty disappointing. I like fried chicken. But other than that Europe is great."
Donnie Wahlberg**

Stir frying is similar to sautéing, but has an important difference. The food you are stir frying is cut into small pieces before frying so it cooks very fast. Less oil is used in stir frying. The goal is to sear and cook each piece of food over high heat so the moisture in the food is retained. After the small pieces food are cooked, a sauce (usually with Asian seasonings) is added to give the dish more flavor and a glazed appearance.

It is challenging to stir fry at home because the heat must remain high, which means you have to move fast. A wok is not designed for a western stove. There is not enough contact to the heat source to keep the entire wok hot. If you stir fry in a sauté pan, make sure all of the ingredients are prepped ahead. Cook in small batches to get the food in and out of the pan quickly and start the next batch while the pan is still hot.

If the heat does not remain high, the ingredients will start to steam rather than fry, and they won't get crispy. If you do not keep the food moving in the pan, it will burn. As with sautéing, cook the food in smaller batches for better results.

"Because normally with Western cuisine, you'll serve vegetables separate from the meat, so kids will eat the meat and never touch the vegetables."
Martin Yan

Deep frying is one method of preparation that so many people love, but they rarely prepare at home. There are self-contained fry machines that have temperature controls that make it easier. This is a good option if you deep fry often and have the room to store it. Lacking that, you can deep-fry in a large pot, but you will need a fry thermometer that registers temperatures in excess of 500°F.

The same tricks and tips apply for deep-fat frying as sautéing and stir frying. Don't crowd the pot with fried items. Monitor the temperature of the oil closely. Remember that water and hot oil don't mix. If the oil should catch fire, smother the flame with a lid or baking soda.

Make sure you have an area set aside with paper towels or a wire rack for the items that are finished frying. Between batches, skim the bits of food and crumbs from the oil as they will continue to cook in the oil, discoloring it and giving it an "off" flavor. The time it takes to "clean" the oil will give it the chance to heat back up to the appropriate frying temperature.

Your exhaust fan is probably not strong enough to keep the fried food smell from permeating your entire house. Your house will smell like fried food for days after. You will also be left with a large amount of used oil that needs to be strained and stored until the next time you deep-fat fry. It is flavored with whatever food you cooked in it.

There needs to be enough oil in the pot for the food to fry without crowding, but not more than half full. When moist food hits the hot oil, it will bubble up. You want it to stay in the pot. When the oil bubbles out of the pot, it will come into contact with the heating surface and can ignite. OK, enough cautionary tales and kitchen disasters.

"I was like any new bride, who said, 'I'm going to cook for my man.' In fact, once I started a small kitchen fire in a pan. Smoke was pouring from the pan, and I got really scared. Right next to our stove is a small fire extinguisher. You know, easy access." Catherine Zeta-Jones

It is time to outline the basics of moist heat methods of preparation. These methods include boiling, braising, stewing, poaching, steaming, and blanching. All of these methods use moisture as a heat conductor to cook food. Some recipes call for a combination of dry heat and moist heat because you cannot brown food using moist heat.

For instance, braising begins by browning the food in a skillet, and then it finishes cooking in a liquid, like stock, water or wine. The caramelized proteins add flavor and color to the liquid that can be used for the sauce or gravy.

When the liquid is added, cover the cooking vessel, and reduce the heat to low so that the liquid is just simmering. Cooking in liquid helps to tenderize those tough pieces of meat that come from the working muscles like the chuck and the round. **With most moist heat methods, low and slow, are the keys to remember.** Very few foods require boiling…it usually makes them tough rather than tender.

Stewing is very much the same as braising. I braise larger cuts, like roasts and I cut the meat into bite sized pieces for a stew, but the method of preparation is the same. I add a thickening agent to the braising liquid for a stew, but not a roast and that would be the difference between stewing and braising.

Poaching is using a liquid like stock, water, juice, wine, or beer and cooking your ingredient by simmering it in the liquid until done. This is not boiling. Poaching is best done with very gentle heat, between 140°F to 180°F. You can poach in the oven or on the stove top depending on the size of the food. Poaching can also be used to infuse color into ingredients.

Steaming is cooking **over** slowly boiling water, rather than **in** the water like poaching. It only takes an inch or two of boiling water to create the steam and cook your ingredient. That is why the water should be at a slow boil. If it is a rolling boil, the water may evaporate completely before your food is cooked. You can use a steamer basket or any rack that will suspend the food over the liquid. When you cover the pot, the steam condenses on the cover, slowing the evaporation of your liquid.

Steaming preserves more nutrients in your food because when you boil, poach or blanch, some of the nutrients will leach out into the water. Then, you pour the vitamins, nutrients, and flavor down the drain. So, steaming is often preferred over poaching. It's also quicker than poaching because you use less water and it comes up to a boil faster.

I blanch vegetables if I want to finish cooking them at a later time. Poach or steam the vegetables briefly and then "shock" them in an ice water bath to stop the cooking right away. If you don't shock them, they will continue to cook because of the residual heat that's inside. The ice bath will bring the temperature right down immediately, preserving the color and texture.

How you choose to cook your food is as important as choosing the food you eat, but it is far more challenging. **Mastering the methods of preparation is what cooking is all about.** In the beginning, chose one ingredient. I suggest chicken because it is inexpensive and versatile. Experiment with different ways of preparing the chicken before you choose another ingredient. Don't forget to use a meat thermometer and find what methods you like best.

> **"When you are at home, even if the chicken is a little burnt, what's the big deal? Relax."**
> **Jacques Pepin**

NOTES

CHAPTER 17

"Show me a man who lives alone and has a perpetually clean kitchen, and 8 times out of 9 I'll show you a man with detestable spiritual qualities."
Charles Bukowski

Food-borne illness is any illness resulting from the consumption of contaminated food. There are close to 50 million incidents every year in the United States. It is more common than you realize, but it is preventable. **Even if you decide not to cook, you should know about food safety.**

Most people don't recognize food poisoning when it happens. In many cases the symptoms are very similar to a cold or the flu. People just feel run down, or queasy. In some cases they may vomit or have diarrhea. Often the symptoms don't appear immediately. It could be hours, days, or even weeks before the onset of symptoms.

The single most important habit to have with regard to food safety is to wash your hands constantly. The enemy is bacteria. One pathogen spoils the food and the other makes people sick. We control the bacteria that spoil food by choosing the best ingredients we can and storing them properly. You can identify the affected food with your senses of sight, smell, touch, and taste. Don't taste tainted food on purpose. "When in doubt, throw it out!"

The pathogenic bacteria that make us sick are harder to detect. They are destroyed by cooking and reheating food to proper temperatures, washing your hands obsessively, sanitizing cutting boards, counters and utensils, and preventing cross contamination. Are these commonly practiced habits in your household?

It is recommended that the temperature inside your refrigerator be colder than 40°F. Keep the temperature below the bacteria danger zone. **Organize your fridge so that raw food (on lower shelves) and cooked food (on higher shelves) is separated.** Don't thaw frozen food on the counter, because it stays in the danger zone longer than it should. Either thaw in the fridge, in the microwave, or in the sink under running water. Use it immediately after thawing.

There's no need to buy an entire line of cleaning products for your kitchen. Dish soap, white vinegar, and bleach are about all you need. Vinegar is a disinfectant and a sanitizing agent when used at full strength. If you dilute bleach with 10 times the water, it is also an effective sanitizer. Washing your hands (for 20 seconds) is the best way to prevent cross contamination in your kitchen. 20 Seconds is a lot longer than you think!

Be especially vigilant when you are cooking for people who are at high risk like the elderly, children, pregnant women, the sick or ill, and those who have an immune deficiency. Realize that I am a chef who is passionate about food, but I'm not a doctor or a nutritionist. If you have questions about food safety, you can get more information on the USDA website www.fsis.usda.gov.

"I don't like food that's too carefully arranged; it makes me think that the chef is spending too much time arranging and not enough time cooking. If I wanted a picture I'd buy a painting."
Andy Rooney

CHAPTER 18

"Get people back into the kitchen and combat the trend toward processed food and fast food."
Andrew Weil

Can you understand why I wrote this book for you? **The greatest benefit I have received from cooking has been the personal connections I have made with others through food.** I hope you get the same appreciation from others that made me fall in love with cooking. The way to anyone's heart is through their stomach!

Share your food. There's nothing like bringing a tray of brownies to the people at the dry cleaners, and seeing the look on their faces as they enjoy them! Share your recipes. My Mother taught me never to go visiting empty handed. Bring a dish and the recipe! Share your stories of success and failure. Everyone who has strapped on an apron (or stained their clothes because they didn't) has stories too. Share your meat chart with someone who is standing there confused in the meat department of the supermarket. There is a lifetime supply of tips and tricks to learn about food and cooking.

I really hope you find some inspiration from this book, and then go into your kitchen and practice once or twice a week with one ingredient at a time and different methods of preparation. Use the kitchen tools you have.

Don't criticize yourself or your food. Learn to cook before you confuse yourself with recipes. Get someone to learn with you, or

at least cleanup after you. Eat your mistakes. Use a meat thermometer. Trust your taste buds. Wash your hands, again. Buy the best ingredients and K.I.S.S.

In "The 4–Hour Chef", Timothy Ferriss listed several hurdles that his Facebook Fans had with learning to cook. They included:

- Too many ingredients (and therefore too much shopping and prep).

- Intimidating knife skills, introduced too early in cookbooks.

- Too many tools, pots, and pans, which are expensive and require too much cleanup.

- Food spoilage.

- Different dishes finishing at different times, leading to cold food, undercooked food, burned food, etc.

- Dishes that require constant tending, stirring, and watching.

I have addressed each of these failure points on these pages. As a way of review, here's my Cliff Notes version:

- Start learning to cook by focusing on ONE ingredient and cooking it using different methods of preparation.

- If you are comfortable with your knife skills, perfect. If not, there is a link to knife skills training in the next chapter.

- I suggest you start with the tools, pots, and pans you already own. If you have nothing, go to a restaurant supply store and outfit your kitchen one piece at a time, starting with your preferred method of preparation.

- You have access to The USDA's "Kitchen Companion: Your Safe Food Handbook" which describes how to shop, store, cook and clean safely.

- You can make sure all your dishes will be done at the same time by learning about methods of preparation using one ingredient at a time, and using a kitchen timer.

- I make no excuses for "dishes that require constant tending, stirring, and watching." Cooking does demand your attention, like any skill you want to learn.

- Get "Cook's Illustrated" and "Fine Cooking" for less than $10 per month. They will be the best home study cooking class you can buy.

I hope reading this book has been a helpful exercise for you. I will give you a link to my website and my email, in case you have any questions along the way. Let me know how I can help you.

NOTES

RESOURCES

"These things are just plain annoying. After all the trouble you go to, you get about as much actual "food" out of eating an artichoke as you would from licking 30 or 40 postage stamps. Have the shrimp cocktail instead." Miss Piggy

Be sure to go to http://ChefMartyRich.com/book-bonus/ and receive your *Secret Ingredients to Successful Cooking.*

Pantry Inventory List Use this printable pantry inventory list to keep up with what's in your pantry, so you never run out of anything, by Erin Huffstetler.

http://frugalliving.about.com/od/stockpiling/ss/Pantry-Inventory-List.htm

2012 Production Guide to Storage of Organic Fruits

and Vegetables More information than you probably want about storing produce properly.

http://nysipm.cornell.edu/organic_guide/stored_fruit_veg.pdf

Meat Charts Weber Smokey Mountain Cooker has an excellent collection of meat charts for beef, pork, lamb, and goat.

http://www.virtualweberbullet.com/meatcharts.html

Pesticide Levels for 45 Fruits and Vegetables
Environmental Working Group's complete list helps you make informed choices about pesticides in produce.

http://www.ewg.org/foodnews/list/

Guide to Seasonal Fruits and VegetablesAn extensive list
prepared by Molly Watson showing what's in season now.

http://localfoods.about.com/od/finduselocalfoods/a/natlseason.htm

Basic Knife Skills Chef Tomm has a couple of YouTube videos that show you basic knife skills.

http://www.youtube.com/watch?v=cV0c7qiNjuI

USDA Food Safety Guide: Kitchen CompanionA
comprehensive guide from the Food Safety and Protection Service explains their 4 step program, Clean, Separate, Cook, Chill.

http://www.youtube.com/watch?v=cV0c7qiNjuI

ChefMartyRich   YouTube   Channel
Three years ago, I recorded a series of videos about Holiday Entertaining leading up to Thanksgiving. Subscribe today! I will be adding more

videos soon.

http://www.youtube.com/user/chefmartyrich

"I go out to the kitchen to feed the dog, but that's about as much cooking as I do." Betty White

Printed in Great Britain
by Amazon

22060556R00062